# UNWHISPERED
# **VOICES**
## A BOOK OF POETRY

DADLO ZUHRANİ

**author**HOUSE

*AuthorHouse*™
*1663 Liberty Drive*
*Bloomington, IN 47403*
*www.authorhouse.com*
*Phone: 833-262-8899*

*Published by AuthorHouse 09/29/2021*

*ISBN: 978-1-6655-3881-7 (sc)*
*ISBN: 978-1-6655-3883-1 (hc)*
*ISBN: 978-1-6655-3882-4 (e)*

*Library of Congress Control Number: 2021919352*

*Print information available on the last page.*

*This book is printed on acid-free paper.*

# DEDICATION

To my father from whom I inherited love of English Language and my mother.

# CONTENTS

# O! ITALY WE STAND WITH YOU

(This poem was written during height
of corona virus in Italy – 2020 when poet was
student at University of Rome, Tor, Vergata)

O! land of mighty emperors
Brave fighters, doughty warriors
Captivating artists, versatile actors
O! Land of art, sculptors, writers
Pope, priests, bishops and Caesars
O! Land of classy fashion designers
In this time of trial and tribulations
Broken hearts and faces crestfallen
Depressed citizens, emotions swollen
O! Italy we stand with you

O! Land of Michael Angelo sculptor
Beautiful people, brave soldiers
O! Land of beautiful hills, lovely valleys
Clean, clear, attractive Roman alleys
Enjoying travelers, revelers' rallies
O! Land of Pastas and pizzas
Ancient mother of innovative ideas
Divine rule clearly tells
Darkness is always brief
We share your unbearable grief
O! Italy we stand with you

If Rome is creeping desolated, so what?
If Milan is weeping isolated, so what?
If Venice is seeping hibernated, so what?
If Florence is sobbing alienated, so what?
O! Country of eternal forbearance
Resilience, rectitude and brilliance

Days are not far away
Deadly Corona is done away
Rome will dance in joy
We all will enjoy
O! Italy, we stand with you

Andrea O! Italian brat
Handsome dashing classmate
Maria woman of high trait
Piga our professor the great
Andrea Appoloni brave upbeat
Corona an ugly monster
With indomitable will, you deter
Italy will stand and conquer
New dawn will be brighter
We the eighth generation of procurers
Your friends, students and guests
Stand with you in hour of test
O! Italy we stand with you.

# REFUGE GIRL

In a frosty chilly night
I a refuge girl, in pitiable plight
Famished, thinned, skeleton like sprite
Losing hope, calm, may die tonight
Come! Come! listen, my harrowing tale
I wish to bare my soul and wail
Hilarious, running, fighting once a gail
Alas golden days, I have lost trail
Inaudible, unusable, invisible, frail
My younghood taken before it came
My dreams stolen before they could beam
To my father I was a precious pearl
Now angst, hate, abuses, each one hurl
Come! Come! listen to me I am a refuge girl

My father, loving, caring, jolly man
To us like an umbrella in rain
My mother, simple, rustic woman
With beautiful hands like woolen
My brother, handsome, hurly burly
Blue eyed, rose colored, hair curly
One day my father came grim faced
Worried, hounded, harassed, afraid
"O!God" there is war cried and said
As time slowly went by
Turning blue into bloody red sky
Bullets, guns, thundering, roaring
Pushing us in fearful mourning
One day early in the morning
They brutal, lethal, came storming
Before we realized what is happening
Alas in the vicious, cruel maddening

I saw, brother, mother, father, killed
I felt, dazed, numbed, despite hair pulled
When I came to sense
Monster mauled me, pain immense
Oho! now I am chattel to whirl
Come! come! listen to me I am a refuge girl

I was sixteen years old
Innocent, gamboling, with a heart of gold
Caught butterflies, ignored fathers' scold
Open spaces my love, me in free mould
Dreamt of a prince while strolled
Handsome, young, dashing, extolled
Alas! My freedom suddenly ended
I was tortured, forced and bedded
I was used, misused, abused, pervaded
I was dishonored, naked and paraded
My screams unheard, tears untended
I am shattered when abuses swirl
Come! come! listen to me I am a refuge girl

I have been, dragged, drawn, thrown
I have been, kicked, picked, strewn
I have been, bruised, butchered, hewn
I have been, jeered, jested, buffoon
I have been, hated, maltreated, spittoon
O! Poet come come near to me
I am hacked, racked hear to me
O busybody little while bear to me

Save soul, my whole body is not alive
Ordeal untellable I will not survive
Now me a pawn in the hands of churl
Come! come! listen to me I am a refuge girl

O! Dejected poet of east
Sitting in Rome in a cozy suite
Leave for a while your feast
Before my eyes cease
Before my lips freeze
Before I stop to breathe
Come to me, listen to me
At the moment of death, I feel
Life unbearable hard ordeal
But I don't want to conceal
I don't want to die
Tell to world my anguished cry
I wish to live and enjoy
I feel my dreams still unfurl
Come! come! listen to me I am a refugee girl.

# MY POETRY IS FOR YOU

O! Free souls, loving birds
Kissing, with warmest words
Embracing, with heartiest hugs
Unwavering, intrepid, lightning bugs
Drowned in each others' eyes
Forgetful of coming separations' signs
O! Couples romantic with tightened lips
O! Friends, lovers with heightened flips
Running, jumping with passion
O! Builders of new dawn, delighted masons
I love thy dreams you pursue
My poetry is for you

O! Nymph, lovely, beautiful, adorned
Thy parting, poet painfully mourned
O! Maiden unaware of my longing
Painful, piercing, breaking, mourning
Days prolonged and are listless
Nights dark, scary and restless
You a girl of ado and glory
Me a poet of worthless story
Oft you come in dreams, in nights
With your lovely regaling sights
Do you remember? you slammed door
Calling me a penniless pauper, a bore
O! My divinely love ordained
You are merciful, I pretend
I am poet lacking chivalry
You beautiful thread, of my story
My poetry is for you

O! Struggling child of the east
Lively, energetic, universe awaits your zest
Awaken your spirit, awaken courage
It is dawn you think a mirage
O! Injured traveler of the caravan
Walk, walk, walk, singing like swan
Courage, consistency shortens distance
O! Child trust historical instance
Who says darkness is your fate?
Who says your plight is doomed state?
O! ye epitome of the courage
Wake and face the world savage
You, hero of unwritten stories
You, hero of forthcoming glories
Shun off thy chaining worry
My poetry is for you

My sage mother my charming wife
One my creator other my life
O! Girl living in city named jewel
Love of olden days without interval
Come, come, meet me I yearn
Before get laid in dark urn
O! Girl living in city of dome
Wealth is your nom de plume
Heroin of my beautiful poem
Keats an immortal poet and sage
TB and longing killed him in young age
He once immortally said
'Beauty is truth and truth is beauty'
O! Beauties of truth and love, I tell you

Me a romantic poet under spell of you
I sing hymns for your youthful flurry
My poetry is for you

My father a dream weaver
My strength, harbor and anchor
You died of brutal cancer
Never forgotten your pain
Screams anguish and strain
Whenever see a man crying
Tears roll down for your suffering
Poverty, life miserable without money
Hard, intolerable path of agony
December eighteen nineteen eighty eight
The day mortal world you left
I weep and recall you under nights starry
Accept tears O! father I am sorry
My poetry is for you…

# STREET URCHIN

Fateful day I cannot forget
Evening, ending time for sunset
One of them came, forcibly took me away
Small, weak, but resisted all the way
They pushed me down, humiliated
Mercilessly beat me and subjugated
Laughed at my anguish wildly incested
Left me worn, torn and abrogated
Repeatedly story goes on
To goons and policemen, I am pawn
O! People living in calm and quiet
Dreaming your children's future bright
Have you ever been victimized?
Have you ever been traumatized?
Have you ever been brutalized?
You cannot understand my pain
Agony, humiliation and sense of shame
O! God why I am a fatherless son?
I am an abused street urchin

For countless nights, I wept, unslept
For countless nights, head smashed
For countless nights, pulled hair unkempt
For countless nights, felt battered, shattered
For countless nights, felt ignored, uncatered
For countless nights, moaned, protested
For countless nights, notion of God resisted
For countless nights, raged, complained
O! God why miserable fate you ordained?
For countless nights, implored, asked
O! God why I am lost and pained?
For countless nights, questioned, called

O! God why I am hated and reviled?
For countless nights, I am hungry, awry
O! God why you forgotten to worry?
O! God why I was born orphan?
I am an abused street urchin

For our ilk is it everywhere same?
In Washington in London in Rome?
Are there same painful stories?
Broken hearts unmanageable worries
Are there same wondering for bread?
Shelter less, loiterers, broken family threads
Are there same, hounding, harassing devils?
Brutal, crushing, unmerciful evils
It is a scorching sunny noon
Aah in the month of June
Sitting under a shadow of wall
Tired of being a rolling ball
I Cry and ask God Almighty
Will there be end to miseries doughty?
Is to be born an orphan a sin?
I am abused street urchin.

# GOOD BYE AUTUMN

While walking on the way
Trees wave and say
We have put on green cloak
O! Poet compose for our look
O! Trees you are happy why?
It is time to say autumn good bye

I greet fairies of Campus X
Walking, talking, playing relax
Thine beauty melts hearts like wax
Mine peace robbed with poetic grace
Thou unaware of lovers' sigh
It is time to say autumn goodbye

O! Mother Earth you have woken
Wintry slumber you have broken
Green dress you have been bestowed
After long wait your glory restored
Your son poet is blushing shy
It is time to say autumn good bye

O! My tall, lovely, singing tree
Poet not knoweth Italian name of thee
Tell me story of happy lovers who say
'O! God save us' stuck in snowy subway
They curse and say autumn be away
It is time to say autumn good bye

O! Tall girl running in the evening
Your beauty is matchless stunning
Walking tracks before sunset
Wait, losing patience and rest
Today why you not on the way?
It is time to say autumn good bye

GOOD BYE AUTUMN

O! Ye wise teach me to tell her
Get close to ear and whisper
My poetry is worthless without you
Come close to me I love you
But me a poet timid and wry
It is time to say autumn good bye.

# FAIRY LIKE GIRL

In my childhood days
My father used to say
About lovely fairy land
Where only bold lovers stay
Heart touching, beautiful story
Cheer up O! girl like fairy

A versatile, born leader
Me, thy friend and admirer
Hey your wine doused hair
Breaks vow abstinent lover
Poet sings thy glory
Cheer up O! girl like fairy

You sing, universe smiles
Let me praise you extra miles
Thou a goddess Aphrodite
Compassionate, considerate, erudite
O! goddess Venus O! goddess Flory
Cheer up O! girl like fairy

Come let us sit under a tree
Angelic girl with soothing smile
I will write poetry for thee
O! inimitable damsel juvenile
Let us while away time eerie
Cheer up O! girl like fairy

While wild roses blossom
God knows you are awesome
You a beckoning lodestar
Folkloric fairy O! polestar
O! freshener in my life weary
Cheer up O! girl like fairy.

# I WRITE TO HIDE MY SCAR.

In the mid of night,
Shining moon, universe bright;
Standing under open sky
Thoughts wild, weep and cry
O! My beloved you left me why?

You were my pride;
My mentor, my guide;
You made my horizon wide;
Now, uncontrollable thoughts chide;
You left me without any reason;
Crucifying me like guilty of treason.

To me; you were future;
Warm sunshine of winter;
Cooler breeze of summer;
Delirious scents of flower;
Precious like pearl hidden;
Now sob of my soul, left; me riven.

You were my beacon of hope;
You were my strength of high scope;
You were ointment when I broke;
Your crushing departure can't cope;
Miseries unending, me pain ridden;
Afflicted with agony burn and brighten.

To be or not to be is not question;
You wrote my bleak fate on horizon;
Each passing day pains widen;
Every day life a pill of poison;
Ooh your memories now frighten!
Want to erase all but longing heighten.

Some say me not poet at par;
I say, I write to hide my scar!
Each moment, life an unconquerable war;
Tears flow, like wine from bowl broken;
I weep, my eyes weary swollen.

A girl holds my hand, says;
'O! God save him' she prays
In her eyes beam love rays
But me, drowned in your craze;
Leave her jilted and bitten;
Eyes imploring, she smitten.

# BRAVO ROMA!

(After prolonged lockdown life in Rome is coming back to normal. This poem is dedicated to my all classmates of IMPPM Tor Vergata specially Sonia, Rym, Shareef, Himawan Giri Dahlan, Makka, Andrea, Maja and Ivana)

After countless days of suffering
Dejection, melancholy and mourning
Aah blew breeze of spring
We came out of shell
Salutations, salams and hails
Bravo Roma! Life is back on trail

Corona! human soul you can wrench
But human spirit you cannot snatch
Jubilation on the streets of Rome
Pronounce your defeat and doom
You have nothing but to wail
Bravo Roma! Life is back on trail

Sweltering sun sends message
Human beings! remember your hard passage
Look at me, sun further talked
I have never tired, never stalked
For only untiring fighters survive
For time immemorial I rise and dive
O! deadly disease you on back foot snail
Bravo Roma! Life is back on trail.

# REFLECTIONS ON THE BANKS OF LAKE BRACCIANO ITALY

Erotic stories written on water
Like wavering thoughts of neophyte lover
My heart sinks for lake Manchhar
To my Sindh a beautiful gift of nature
O! You victim of greed and abhor
Poet weeps for your erstwhile grandeur

Beneath green mountain
O! Bracciano, majestic beauty you retain
You behold right, for love in first sight
Poet is convinced and certain
To him poetry flows like fountain

Milky girls lying like statue frozen
Poet feels from rose petals you made in
O! friend Shareef Amosh why are you broken?
O! Princesses of fragrance, Shareef's heart is raven

Two girls alluring, floating on yacht
So lovely their company to be sought
But heart of poet is filled with fear and fraught
For many days you dazzled my thought

Far above the lake there is cloud
Pining to cover you from sunny side
Drizzle, it sends on heavenly ride
Cloud in love stands you along side

On your banks, I recall Jasmine
Fragrance of eternity, quest of mine
O! gift of God, O! my souls' sign
Before twilight of life, shower your shine

O! European beauty with green eyes
I wrote poem for you as a surprise
O! My comforting queen wise
You make sinking hearts rise

O! European beauty! O! Roma's rage!
Poet is timid and lacks courage
To you his poems are a message
Oft in morning his peace you ravage

O! Arfa my wife charming
Thine husband writes poetry heartwarming
Philanderer though he is, but not harming
On lake romantic he is heeding your warning.

# I WILL NOT DIE - STORY OF A CALL GIRL.

I wonder if you are my father!
A leech, a man of mean character
Have killed me before birth, was better
You waited for my maturity
Sold me the day I got puberty
You took me to cut your deal
Oblivious to my pain that I feel
My buyers said 'he counts money and cheers'
But I was lost how to count my tears

Before my strength awoke
Shackles you put me broke
I was woken by divinely stroke
A new page of life I wrote
I was called a call girl
Made to dance and swirl
Pimp a father a churl
O! God what humiliations you hurl?

I refused to sell my soul furthermore
I refused to obey you O! father of whore
I refused to be torn anymore
I felt sorry I couldn't it before
You worried for your bruised pride
Made me hungry, locked me inside
Unbent now, woken soul my guide
'Kill me' in frustration you decide

You treated me your field
Harvesting to earn your yield
Me a soulless entity for your greed
You O! man of vicious breed
Your fertile field is gone

O! Merciless killer O! Butcher born
You will beg for a grain of corn
Now you will be stock for scorn

The day you killed me with axe
I did not cry, enjoyed your hacks
Flew off to sky, body torn with cracks
My departure calm and composed
But your peace shattered, you decomposed
Restless like ghost yearning to be dozed
A villain of story in future to be perused

You think it against eastern pride
You detest poem and deride
Pity my father and take his side
'Poet wrote a dirty poem' you snide
From the sky I testify
Pen of poet is drenched in my blood ridden cry
In my sobs and unheard sigh
Immortalized in poem now I will not die.

# O! MY BELOVED

In far off mountains Sun dips low
Hurrying to kiss beloved waiting below
Trying to honour loyalty vow
Me too come from far off land
Made of mountains, river, ocean, sand
Wished to kiss your hair, dimples and feet
My action till resurrection I will repeat

In a sweltering sunny noon
Standing on a burning dune
As the grains of sand shine
I feel you singing under tree of wine
Now desert turning into heaven
O! My beloved you are chosen by divine
You are my nectar is proven

O! My beloved me from a land
Greetings through moon we send
In the night in dazzling light
Walking in street moonlit bright
If you feel tender touch on cheek
On your lips trickles smile meek
Moonlight is kissing you on behalf of lover freak.

# I AM LIVING WITH A HOPE.

I am living with a hope ......
My country blooming without yoke
No more any uncouth's stifling stroke
My poems read, without tyrants choke
I am living with a hope

I am living with a hope.......
When human beings will respect each other
Sufferings and sorrows, love and joy, share together
No one to be killed for his, race, religion and colour
From east to west, south to north, no anguish but cheer
Human brotherhood not subject to whims of a crook
I am living with a hope

I am living with a hope.........
I will not be killed by atom bomb
Or be stoned by a blood thirsty mob
Or be stilled by a cynical snob
Or sustain bullet of army soldier or brutal cop
Tolerant free world without nuke
I am living with a hope

I am living with a hope...........
I am not forced to toe your line
I am not coerced to give up freedom sign
I am not ordered my identity to consign
I am not bothered what individuality I assign
Born free, ideas freely evoke
I am living with a hope

I am living with a hope.,
You don't reject me, if I am distraught
You correct me, if I am out of thought
You protect me, if I am vulnerability fraught

You reflect me, if I am pain wrought
A divinely gifted humanity we can't revoke
I am living with a hope........

I am living with a hope....
If one is killed in Asia, other is riled in America
If one is thrilled in Australia, other is filled in Eurasia
If one is hailed in Africa, smile is holy grail of Makka
If one is railed in Latin America, other wailed in south Asia
Let us love for each other invoke
I am living with hope........

I am living with a hope.......
You will come to me and say ae hey
O! Poet I long for you all the day
Let us recite poetry keep pain at bay
Embrace me I am under poetic sway
Tie me in loves' rope
I am living with a hope........

I am living with a hope.........
Before my soul departs to world other
Fear, greed, angst, hatred I wish to conquer
O! God purify me like holy water
Soul blessed; heart unstained pure
To me life a ceaseless probe
I am living with a hope........

I am living with a hope.............
On my final day angels will come and say
A poet's life comes to end he wished the way
Son, wife, jasmine with tears good bye they say
Mortal body immortal soul your journey comes to nay
In darkness I will not grope
I am living with a hope........

# O! BEAUTIFUL GIRL EUROPEAN!

Your beauty wakes heavenly imagination
Poetic seed breaks, bursts into fermentation
Tranced ecstasy awakes, and feel jubilation
O! Sarswati of creativity, O!
Lakshmi of creation
O! Beautiful girl European!

When your eyes blink
Poetry implores me to think
Ballads, sonnets, odes hurry to wink
Write, write, write O! poet hunk
Mirroring thy fragility my thoughts caution
O! Beautiful girl European!

Your finger in mouth, element of surprise
Not once, not twice, look up at you thrice
Your smile to me, expensive gift and prize
Now sadness I banish, and gloom chastise
Your beauty flowing like waves from ocean
O! Beautiful girl European!

Your tongue on dried slim lips
As if drenched with honey dips
Moves earth and sky, my heart rips
Before I drink, feel quenched with wine sips
Stop please, don't play with my emotions
O! Beautiful girl European!

You elegant like flowers bloom
You vibrant like clouds roam
You concordant like music of stream
With grace strident like stars beam
Words worth's daffodils greet you turn by turn
O! Beautiful girl European!

Dimple in your cheeks, my feeling sweeps
Longing to kiss you, within heart creeps
Revelation of poem, reward poet reaps
I dream for you O! lovely in my sleeps
O! ye universe made for your fun
O! Beautiful girl European!

# ROME AT NIGHT

It is delight to be in Rome at night
Beauty in the night, above imaginations' flight
Damsels of tall height, for poet mesmerizing sight
Lovers' folded arms tight, poetic vision they ignite
Swirling beauties generate new thought
Poem, 'Rome at night' I will write
It is delight to be in Rome at night

Lips are hooked, cheeks kissed like holy book
Inhaled and breaths puffed, stilled eyes love struck
Bravo covid caveat rebuffed, emotional pleasure chuck
Wow brave people toughed, fear stifled, hatred buck
Aah what a scene brilliant bright
It is delight to be in Rome at night

Humans of bone and flesh, undeterred by any caveat
Unmatchable bravery splash, untailored to word retreat
Stood aloft not to crash, unfettered to invisible threat
O! enemy hidden we are brash, to us you can't browbeat
Look at glasses filled with wine red and white
It is delight to be in Rome at night

Moon comes down on earth, blessed girls its new birth
The glittering stars' worth, revealed by blissful mirth
O! jasmine what you doth? Don't you feel fragrance coming forth
Muezzin from tower says, Rome is not for uncouth
You a paradise for beauty lovers, upright
It is delight to be in Rome at night

O! Rome Europe's jewel, on your streets Sonia Rim to revel
A brand of pupilage loyal, Andrea Shareef Giri at night marvel
Bek's two princess's royal, cute witty babies dazzle
Joyous Other stock joyful, Bart, Emman, Zumard, to babble
To me you are love at first sight
It is delight to be in Rome at night.

# A POET IN PAIN

He writes poems for girl living in far off land
Long way in her love he has to wend
He uses words, sentences to extol beauty grand
Poems for every twelve years every Friday he sends
Stone hearted beloved, her heart never bends
Once in blue moon, call she attends
Poet consoles, for him, still she cares and tends
Then a master piece in her praise is written
Alas a poet is in pain

You think, poet is useless stuff
He comes for you and you bluff
You a beautiful, he a man rough
You an immortal, he like a puff
O! Long haired Jasmine, O! My pink colored wine
Care for poet's pine, he is your love divine
The day he will die, you will weep, why?
You realize gone is your lover superb high
Your tears after his departure
Are for love you wish to recapture
But he will not come again
Alas a poet is in pain.

# THANK FRIEND YOU KEPT ME ALIVE.

I am poet hanging upside down
In the mid of night kidnapped by unknown
They kick me in ribs abuse and frown
Stop writing poems or will be cut down
O! Poet disloyal to sacred crown
O! Poet of betrayal prove your allegiance
Merciful king will forgive your negligence
You will be pardoned for your intransigence
King will grant you gifts and prize
Your fortune will rise above your capacity and size
With swollen lips and broken hips
I wish to speak with lisps and hiccups
O! Powerful agents of mighty king
Shudder to your hearts my poetry brings
Now if you kill me or crucify
My friends sing my poetry I will survive
Oho! Thank friend, you kept me alive

Other day my mother came and said
They came and cousin of yours kidnapped
Molested women in nightly raid
Mom warmly kissed my forehead
Uttered words very sad
O! My son don't think to run
Write your poems and have fun
When they take you away
'My son was poet' I will say
He loved me and country same way
Aah soul of my son you will never sway
I know his poetry will make him revive
Oho! Thank friend, you kept me alive

I write poems for nightingale to sing
I write poetry that happiness brings
I write poetry for young hearts to swing
I write poetry for depressed not to cringe
My poetry to gods of earth is biting sting
For crime of mine writing poesy
I am declared criminal of heresy
I am destined for no mercy
A poet of people will be killed today
Silence silence silence all the way
My body will be thrown on sideway
My mutilated body will strive
Spirit of my compatriots will thrive
Oho! Thank friend, you kept me alive

Makka my dear friend
In the country of king, it is trend
Kill those who don't bend
Read my message which I send
O! My dear friend Makka
Custodian of culture of Georgia
When they kill me and I die
Turn this poem into drama high
I will come from sky
From the beams of light come to you nigh
Sit to see you direct and cry
In a free European country
It is my joy and victory
They failed to kill me, bye
Oho! Thank friend, you kept me alive.

# SONG OF SEPARATION- A NEW BORN GIRL

O! my man my honor my fame
Memorable day in my life you came
Filled with love, passions aflame
More beautiful and blessed girl I became
You roused within me hidden ember
Burning me like dry timber
You were my handsome lover sane
O my man....

For you my eyes never wore
Long wait made them not to sore
Hustle bustle felt furor
You were my king coming from off shore
My boat of love sank
I felt ditched and blank
Why I am in such a shame and pain?
O my man ........

Before my life went into shambles
In east on bike, you rode me in trembles
In west in metro and many other vehicles
You knew me like a suspense novel's preamble
Alas now I am a book torn apart
My pain my grief never to depart I am a girl slain
O my man..............

You played with me like a doll
A notebook to unreadable words scrawl
I wish I could know O! untrustworthy pal
You wished to tear me apart and haul
Now I am depressed and sunk
For you O! disloyal hunk Why I wail and mourn?
O my man..............,

Do you remember In Rome near fountain
A poet read poem for visitors to entertain
Reference to separation found to contain
A grief stricken girl tears could not retain
You hugged me and said
I will never leave you don't be afraid
For your deception I find no reason
O my man................

Now in long lonely nights wintry
Loneliness makes me sulky
Growl of wolves I feel for you spunky
And barking of dogs makes me grumpy
Now I think for you why shall I mourn
Memories of past shall I scorn
You a scoundrel of narrow vision
O my man..........

You fiddled my hair and played
Toasted for me and cheered
Unconditional love claimed and relayed
For you, me a divinely art piece to be displayed
But now a girl no more to be cared
Useless piece for no attention deserved
Divinely art piece shattered and torn
O my man..........

Other day in a slaves' land crackled
I saw a wise man's grave shackled
For posterity he willed his grave not unshackled
Until dawn of freedom his land is free unshackled

Aah his will to me is a beckon
Now my pain I can better reckon
A new way I have been shown
O my man..........

In wintry midnight, flare I feel within
For unworthy to end life, I shouldn't
To forget not to regret, why I couldn't?
Now joy of life will I greet, earlier hadn't
Now I am brave girl to fight and stand
Bye sorrows, grief I will withstand
I will be a girl new born
O my man .....................

# DREAM GIRL

Thousands miles away from home
On a chilly night landed in Rome
I searched for a car
Language proved a big bar
I thought I will die!

Isolated, forlorn, Campus X
Harassed, haunted, pale, desolate
Staff behaved like czars
Fear added to my scar
I thought I will die!

A cloudy chilly morning
I saw you walking
I felt sense of rainbow
To your beauty wished to bow
I thought I shall not die!

Walking on a cooler noon
I felt at Vatican zone
Honking of cathedral bell
Announces era of your spell
I thought I shall not die!

Black mole on your cheek
Obsession of a freak
Life will come to deceased
Hearing your voice a feast
I thought I shall not die!

Tiber smoothly flowing
Visualize your face glowing
In your eyes, sorrows drown
Your sights, tremble crown
I thought I shall not die!

Your nose, tip of beautiful rose
Your lips, line of beautiful prose
You speak sweeter than lark
My heart feels a spark
I thought I shall not die!

Your hair shining and pearly
Brisk beautiful lovely and curly
O! Golden girl of vitality
You are unmatched reality
I thought I shall not die!

Your feet, flowery and supple
You walk earth feels chuckle
O! Girl made of jasmine
You are a precious goldmine
I thought I shall not die!

Your beauty angels smile
Long to see you once in a while
O! lovely girl of beautiful land
Make me fresh and agile
I think I shall not die!

Thou beauty of the west
Me a poet of east
Can we meet?
Seems an endless quest
I thought I shall not die!

# LET US DANCE

(Written during the inauguration ceremony of the 8th
Generation of IMPPM University of Rome, Tor, Vergata)

Spring is coming
Birds chirping and singing
Calling for beauty and trance
Let us dance!

Sharif and Emman
Noble Souls of Amman
Harbingers of new dawn
Let us sing like swan
Let us dance!

Rym and Sonia
Two gems of Tunisia
Beauty of Rome you tell
You a pair of gazelle
Let us dance!

Aytikan, Zumard, Makka
Three jewels of Eurasia
Three belles of sobriety
Talents of wide variety
Let us dance!

Andjela and Ivana
Two Serbian stars
Like lovely tune of guitar
Be our avatar
Let us dance!

Andrea, Bart, Sasa, Vadim
Men of honor and esteem
Fill your flask of wine
Listen to nature's rhyme
Let us dance!

From the land of fairytales
Ulghbeg, Koseyn, Sabit hail
Snow is coming to cease
Mirth and joy to increase
Let us dance!

Zeljika, Zorika, Sabina
Precious pearls of Bosnia
With poetic gait
Beautiful, lovely, ornate
Let us dance!

Beautiful blonde Maja
Adriatic bliss of Croatia
With your mellifluous voice
Let us cheer and rejoice
Let us dance!

Lovely Far East Asia
Sober Giri of Indonesia
Java is smiling joyous
Honest, upright, enormous
Let Us dance!

Ya! Cheikhna ya pal!
Thorough Scholar of Senegal
Spring makes Autumn to shake
Africa is drowsy and awake
Let us dance!

# ROME, WE MISS YOU!

(Written during the peak lock down time in Rome)

Morning you are a poet's dream
Noon you are a novelists' stream
Evening you are a musicians' scream
The night you are a singers' theme
O! Rome we miss you

Some of us despaired and are gone
Some of us are burdened to carry on
Some of us bored, distressed, drawn
Some of us secluded, sorrowful, forlorn
O! Rome we miss you.

# ANTHEM OF 8TH GENERATION IMPPM

(This poem was written during the lockdown; classes were switched to online. We' were confined to campus of University of Rome, Tar, Vergata)

We were shackled and fettered
We were hackled and hindered
But our strong resolve undeterred
We cried, laughed and read
But message of love we spread
For the forbearance we were retailers
We were eight th generation procurers

O! Country of thousand bells
Filled with fragrance of jasmine to inhale
In beauty natural you excel
Oho! country of beautiful girls frail
Accept our greetings love and hails
To us thou a host of fine caliber
We were eight th generation procurers

Some of us were sad and dejected
Some of us were lonely and berated
But despair, all of us rejected
Melancholy never let to be overstated
We never let the spirit to weaken
And never let valor to be shaken
We were love seekers, love purchasers
We were eight th generation procurers

For four months every day
We stuck to screens and say
We have kept our sorrows away
Stories were told by our eyes

By the lips by lovely smiles,
We felt each other strongly
Strong emotions, feelings lovely
We were untiring warriors
We were eight generation procurers

Andjela your soothing smile
Maja your sobering profile
Aytikn, Zumard your childlike style
Makka my friend versatile
Rym and Sonia your leading guile
Zorica our friend with mind fertile
You all were flag bearers
We were eight th generation procurers

O! Ivana sober girl Serbian
Lovely Emman of Jordan
Zeljka hilarious with heart golden
Sabina charming beauty Bosnian
Of light and elegance, you torch bearers
We were eight th generation procurers.

From Afghanistan Behzad Sabeti
May God grant your country prosperity
O! Giri man of multi variety
Honored man of piety
Smiling face free of anxiety
Of grace you were sellers
We were eight th generation procurers

Bart and Vadim our vectors
Philosopher guides in weak sectors

Sasa lover of healing nectars
Jordanian Sharif a love creator
Andrea O! ye our beloved tutor
You all removers of barriers
We were eight th generation procurers

Centre of class Cheikhna of Senegal
Sabit, Ulubeg our valuable pals
Bek father of cute babies who enthrall
Professors Piga, Annalisa saved us from fall
Cristina you our savior in seasons all
You saved us from sadness and failures
We were eight th generation procurers

Our friendship deeper than oceans
Far beyond and above worldly notions
Me a poet of South Asian origins
For my poetry you a vast horizon
I will miss you O! my lovely dears
We were eight th generation procurers.

# A WHITE GIRL IN THE ARMS OF BLACK MAN

Round me and wrap me up
Drowse me with kisses and hugs
Hold me in your hands lift me up
Let us tell the world, hate, love shrugs

When you kiss me joyous am I
On your chest when I sleep
Unaware of eyes of astonished passers by
In my heart nothing but your love beeps

O! Strangers with prying eyes
My black-man, for me first drizzle of summer rain
Warmth of his love make you vie
O! My scholar intellectual O! worthy man sane

By your side O! My love black
I am chilled and fulfilled
Your absence makes my heart crack
In your presence I am thrilled

On the height of mountain green
You point to beauty of lake mingling with sky
But O! my beloved I'm lost in your love and sheen
Your beauty eternal, rest I nullify

I recall the day first
I was mesmerized by eyes black
I lost my peace, my rest
The day I felt you are my birthday cake

Love is above caste, creed, colour
Love is invisible light for the blind
Love makes me chaste and I valour
Purified am I purified is my mind.

# COME TO ME

Life's journey is coming to end
Life, thorny hitting, wish with you to blend
O! my lover O! my befitting friend
No space for time rebutting, how to amend?
O! my love lost I am fallen and sad
For your separation unbearable price paid
Grieved, anguished, impossible to stand
I recall day I a bride newly wed
Oblivious to your pain and tears you shed
I remember farewell you did with bowed head
You were my love but I yearned for lovely life ahead
You O! poor writer, flung words like cascade
Words for me you used and praised
Your simplicity I couldn't evade
Your sincerity aah I was impressed
You will write poems, stories and novel
Me your companion, dreamt to marvel
Alas everything went away asunder
Chose upon you a wealthy vendor
Now life is deceiving me
Slowly slowly leaving me
O my friend hold my hand come to me
I am dying, for you crying, come to me
Come to me .......

I left him he left me
New wife the day he got
With paper of divorce, he left me wrought
For ten years like vulture, he ate me

With mental torture, he wrapt me
Blackened my future, he beat me
Uncouth, unaware of refined culture,
chained he kept me, oho unbearable torture
I told my painful story to mother
And my stone hearted Sister
Aah to me came advise, bear!
If you a divorcee, will be like used tin of beer
Discarded per se, worthless for later
No one will show mercy, my daughter remember
Against him to stand you see, a mistake very clear
O! my poet O! My novelist O! my lover of days gone
I couldn't resist, I couldn't desist, I lonely forlorn
On every step, I lost respect, I suddenly was worn
O! my love my hope, in darkness I grope
Come to me like light, make me to excite
You cheered me when I was sad
You jeered at my fear, when I was afraid
Darkness in the tunnels end, for light why shall I fend?
To death vulnerable, for life why shall I stand?
But I have wish, before I perish
Come to hold my hand so I say
My end is not scary
O! my lover come to me, come to me.

# AM I LOST?

Sometimes I feel biting frost
Other times reel under heat vast
Is time slow or moving fast?
Unaware about worthy past
Below earth, where am I?
Or flowing up in sky?
Where me have to stop?
Am I missed or am I lost?

Tongue of mine wounded
For singing songs was rounded
My eyes taken out
For looking at mighty stout
Konweth not about
For the other bodily rout
For singing paid heavy cost
Am I missed or am I lost?

Parrot was I not
Forgot to talk what was taught
In my songs word "Freedom" brought
Angry master said O! "rebel" what?
Cross, he was filled fraught
To sing for master, sorry I forgot
Death for my slip I got
Am I missed or am I lost?

Holding my picture, I feel mother
Vision of my wife tears blur
My sister injured with slur
My eight year son shivers in fear
Longing, separation with tear
Gloom gloom gloom pal is cast

For me I know my land is downcast
Am I missed or am I lost?

Am I dead or am I killed?
Or destined as God willed
Or for my free thinking billed
For my dreams that thrilled
Yearning for freedom, so grilled
Thrown, kicked and whirled
No one helped aah in world vast
Am I missed or am I lost?

Mighty has forbidden
My name shall not be taken
My friends afraid and shaken
But O! poet thine spirit you awaken
For me your poem written
Will console my mother broken
And stir the sleepy to waken
I am a soul not to be cast
Am I missed or am I lost?

# O! LOVELY GIRL SWEET

O lovely girl sweet
For you my heart beats
Your face as if a new dawn greets
You a blazing star complete
To me polite discreet
O! Lovely girl sweet

Holding your hand supple
My heart dances and feels ripple
Ticking of clock freezes to standstill
Gone my sorrows run to cripple
You are sweet I wish to repeat
O! Lovely girl sweet

Your flowing hair long
Wondering Black clouds to sky belong
Minted in Jasmine if I am not wrong
Waving like a rivers' current strong
Not to waste time come to meet
O! Lovely girl sweet

I will not bring stars from sky
And precious stones from mountains dry
Jewels from the deep sea worldly beauty belie
And hollow promises unable to comply
O! My shadow in sweltering sunny heat
O! Lovely girl sweet

If you are not my soulmate
Why visions poetic thoughts create?
And your name rouses emotions upbeat
Your notions sudden my poems fret
Land is beautiful where you put feet
O! Lovely girl sweet.

# MAKKA I MISS YOU

To Tablisi I will come
O! My friend beautiful awesome
With a glass of wine, gin or rum
Will hold your hand and read poem fulsome
In a western country met you worthy friend
You caught my mind, heart and poetry down to end
First rays of eastern dawn kiss you
Makka I miss you

In the lonely nights of Rome
Poetic thoughts rush to come
Every poem without you was unwelcome
Your reference makes poetry wholesome
To me you beacon of light
A poet's tender feelings you ignite
My pen, my poetry reminisce you
Makka I miss you

Will you take me to a vineyard?
Sit by my side and listen to bard?
Grapes be our shadow and guard
O! my lovely companion girl of high regard
To me you are friend or beloved?
For you I feel love in my blood
I wish to bliss you
Makka I miss you.

# YOU ASK ME TO PROVE MY LOYALTY

Before my tongue slips
O! My lord I sewed my lips
I force my thinking mind
I am human never me to remind
O! my Lord of descent royalty
Still you ask me to prove my loyalty?

Before your gun clicks
My tongue my wounds licks
Other day my son was killed
With grief up to hill was filled
Yet I didn't weep on your cruelty
Still you ask me to prove my loyalty?

Filled with sorrows but they are not mine
God has created all happiness for thine
What comes to my life doesn't matter
Your glory must go from great to greater
Me on earth ugly creature filthy
Still you ask me to prove my loyalty?

On a forsaken land I was sent
On shining of your shoes millions are spent
To be loyal to your shoes is my aim prime
Your uniform is precious you are sublime
My rags and my soul are to clean shoe dirty
Still you ask me to prove my loyalty?

All those you have punished
With scale of justice crushed
What if they were my brothers and sisters
Emotionless am I they are not worthy of tears
Why they stood against you I feel guilty
Still you ask me to prove my loyalty?

At the end of night dew is a tear
Shed by sky in your horror and fear
For you my lord never will I say so
For all words that against you go
 O! my lord trust my fealty
Still you ask me to prove my loyalty?

Wrong are all who say
Cruelty is end of the way
For all darkness a new dawn is to rise
For the cruel with a hidden surprise
O! my lord you will not suffer for your brutality
Still you ask me to prove my loyalty?

# I WILL FIGHT UNTIL I DIE

I will stand and fight until I die
A vow, a warrior's cry
With will unfaltering spirit high
Until for my people limit is sky,
I will stand and fight until I die

If you think you will hound me
With your bullshit pound me
With your power will ground me
Mistaken you are with your whims
A burning light within me stems
For my people I am battle cry
I will stand and fight until I die

If you think you are invincible
You a mighty and untouchable
You a mountain me a variable
Come out of your hallucinations
Day dreams are your fascinations
For battered me a fighter guy
I will stand and fight until I die

I have no gun to show
Neither money to stow
Nor any present to bestow
I write poems to inspire
My words live wire
My pen a weapon you can't buy
I will stand and fight until I die

Me a son of beautiful soil
My parentage believer in toil
Unbreakable spirit none can foil

Phoenix like are we
From ashes stand to face thee
Our courage you can't deny
I will stand to fight until I die

Who wins or loses is not question
Between wrong and right what is distinction
With right I will make an impression
Even in defeat I will be a hero
Hero of hope not like you a zero
My ideals death will magnify
I will stand and fight until I die.

# YOUR MEMORY MAKES ME HAPPIER

Stars are twinkling and moon in bloom
Desperate is my heart in pall of gloom
Jumbled are thoughts, weary, fail to groom
Aah my life surrounded by multi syndrome
Suddenly I see hope flickers
O! my friend your memory makes me happier

Burning is body even with sweat
But your memory O! girl sweet
Pain is gone and sorrow is to retreat
Strong am now for sadness to beat
Feeling happiness of a revelers
O! my friend your memory makes me happier

Alas! in the middle of night, a cry I hear
A cry that my heart will tear
A mother is trembling in fear
From the hungry babies' stare
But your vision comes from somewhere
O! my friend your memory makes me happier

In my village as if I am in hell
Neither calm nor comfort, I feel
Thoughts jumbled overtaken me to dwell
O! God send us a soothing spell
Wow gust of wind comes like your whisper
O! my friend your memory makes me happier

Soft feel of your hands beautiful
In the heat killing, makes life colourful
You are my fresh air I am not doubtful
To kiss your eyes is a dream to fulfil
To me you are becoming nice to nicer
O! my friend your memory makes me happier

For all the love you have given
No regret now if life is done
Thanks to you for the life I have been
All the honours of world I have won
O! Beauty lovely now I feel better
O! my friend your memory makes me happier

Thousands miles away you are
But from my heart you are not far
I see you in the sky O! my life's star
To me in summer hot a tree cedar
To me O! my beloved nectar
O! my friend your memory makes me happier.

# ON THE SUICIDE OF A LADY DOCTOR IN KARACHI

You took away your own life
O! beautiful girl with ambitions high
I am unaware of your inner strife
But saddened you ended life why?

Beauty, God bestowed you with gift
And born with silver spoon
What tore you apart and created rift
So you lost hope and divinely boon?

O! beautiful girl like rainbow
Your beauty inspiration for many
For lover you a human to bow
No time for you to end life shiny

Neither I know you O! girl beautiful
Your departure has touched heart of mine
Tender feelings you ignited to hearts grateful
A poet's heart is shaken on death of thine

Beauty is truth Keats said
I believe in the words of master
But your suicide belies the adage
Death was not for you but a life sweeter

Universe weeps when a beautiful woman dies
A beautiful woman truth of universe
A beauty's death earth mourns and sky cries
Wonderful gift is life but not a farce.

# RUMBLINGS

To take your name is forbidden
In shaken country fear ridden
You exponent of truths hidden
You a hope for slaves downtrodden

You sleeping in grave of marble white
O! beacon of hope you took us to height
To enemy your name symbol of shaking fright
To us you are hope O! Saen innocent upright

In a country of people harassed
Of cruelty all limits are crossed
For the pleasure of king heads are chopped
Heads of rebels kicked and tossed

Other day a girl left for lover
Abused her mother and father
four years later honeymoon over
Ditched by lover now a beggar

Sages say love is gift of divine
My heart broken my love you decline
For me without you nothing is fine
Not a gift but love is pain pristine

I miss your laughter, looks and smile
Your charm, heart warm and lovely style
On your lips my feelings I wish to file
But reality and fiction does not reconcile

Alas I have no feathers no wings to fly
To convey my love to you on poems rely
Unconditional love of mine you deny
Wait is unending but still you do not reply

My love has always been like a child orphan
from door to door up for mercy of anyone
All the doors are locked I live under illusion
You are not mine but I am happy with delusion

We will meet someday somewhere
With open arms will greet each other
In each other's arms joyous together
Pray for time to stop for lasting get together

I have to tell you a horrific tale
About a mother weak and frail
Her son's soul was not for sale
He was killed in bloody assail

To you I secretly admire and worship
For all thy glory my passion flares up
Your longing has overtaken me with grip
Longing is killing, separation hastens to rip.

# RICH IS RICHER AND POOR IS POORER

Rich is richer and poor is poorer
Destiny of rich is from sure to surer
Alas poor is from poor to pauper
No hope for him from any corner
Crush him is the day's order

In a dirty hut road along side
Harassed is sitting a bride
Father worried how to tears hide
For her pain mother gonna swide
Farewell to daughter is ordeal harder
Rich is richer and poor is poorer

One week before marriage her father was called
By the powerful mighty in a beautiful house walled
A man horrible offered daughter's beauty to be mauled
A price suitable for the burden of life to be overhauled
A father wished to die then and there
Rich is richer and poor is poorer

O! God how shall I describe pain of people?
Begging for bread even though skilful
Worried how to save their daughters beautiful
Hearts grief ridden eyes smitten with tales doleful
O! God I am lost utterly miserable mourner
Rich is richer and poor is poorer

Children in rags barefooted with dreams lost
Their childhood looted hopes gone in poverty's blast
Needs are hooted but miseries uncountable avast
Life is is not lived but series of unbearable thoughts
May I still call this world colourful soberer?
Rich is richer and poor is poorer

I write poems but for what and for whom?
For those whose youth ends before bloom?
Or for the lovers lost in poverty's eternal gloom?
Waiting for valentines but pain grows like mushroom
Is there end to this doom clearer?
Rich is richer and poor is poorer

Me am neither a narcissist nor an unbeliever
My God! Lovely, I see around not a single healer
Humanity is suffering send us a soothing feeler
Before shaken is faith of a staunch believer
Hope shall not be lost for far ever
Rich is richer and poor is poorer.

# PAIN OF A WEEPING MOTHER

A weeping mother from crushed land
Holding photo of son before press club stands
"My son a teacher' she wails and tells
Last night kidnapped and daughter injured by bullet shells
He was brave boy, wrote poetry sang with joy
His dreams flew high, between earth and sky
Alas he has been taken away
I wait for the day
When I will get his bullet ridden body
Till then come to me, before reality frightens me
In a moment awesome, pain is tiresome
Come to me share my pain
Pain of a son slain
Son slain by inane
Inane wearing clothes plain
Inane cruel in their domain
Inane prone to killings insane

For all the mothers living in far off lands
I wish to send message
High still my head stands
But I am mother grief ridden
Openly to weep for me is forbidden
I am asked never to ask
For my son taken by men in mask
I am mother to forget son, I lack dare
In torture cell you are but where?
O! Mothers living world wide
Share my grief before my son is died
Come to me let us pain divide

For my son I implore you
Raise your voice I swore you

Your voice will make a big bang
They will be afraid for son to hang
Thankful to thee I will be
Tranquil to a degree I shall be

Alas in the books of history it is written
All pain freedom fighters' mothers have been
Their sons are killed only once
But mothers die daily for heart burns
Martyrs are hope for the millions
And dream dreadful for the villains
For pain of a mother imagine
Who receives son's body bullet ridden
If you think justice is everywhere
Mistaken you are, dark patches are there
In Asia cruelty is multi sphere
Against the brutality I write poetry
For me it is crusade until victory
My friends come share my ideals
Before your friend is gone to world unreal.

# I WILL NOT LET MY PEOPLE DOWN

You ask me to kneel down
Before your sacred crown
No I will not O! King brown
I will not let my people down

Suffering people they are
To them you are a sacred avatar
But peace to them is very far
Their sufferings I will own
I will not let my people down

Before they break In your fear shake
Think for the cause to forsake
My poems will not let morale down
I will not let my people down

I believe pen never fails
If it fails my blood will bring new spell
My unbowed head will tell new tale
Damn care for your angry frown
I will not let my people down

Just living is not name of life
To loath tyranny is actual frame of life
Kneeling down is factual shame of life
I want to die like brave soldier known
I will not let my people down

Billions are living on earthen globe
But a few stand out amongst huge mob
A few valiant souls for whom hearts throb
Noble souls by whom new way is shown
I will not let my people down.

# I HAVE FEELINGS

I have feelings wrapped in red rose
Poetic saplings or line of beautiful prose
Flying butterfly or bird colourful I suppose
Stars twinkling or wonderful moonlight flows
River peaceful or powerful spring goes
I have feelings..............

I have feelings
To come to you and tell you story
Of my misery, poverty and life gory
Share my grief and lessen worry
For me you feel grieved and sorry
Locked is your door, where pain to repose?

I have feelings........

I have feelings
I recall the moment you came to me
Aah your hair flowing enflame me
Thy cheeks glowing aflame me
Powerless was I don't blame me
To your beauty a toast I propose?
 I have feelings........

I have feelings
My heart is aching my eyes swollen sore
Your memory breaking, pain never seen before
I a rudderless, away, off base, drowned off shore
I a thirsty, glass is empty, but to you still adore
All the lovers, faithful followers, are to dispose
I have feelings...........

I have feelings
My life story is very discordant and brief
Of lost love and filled with abundant grief
Of emotions distraught torn redundant leaf
Of scattered thoughts caught in fervent disbelief
I have to live and just to live as a morose
I have feelings...........................

I have feelings
For a country of mountains green
Girls' beauty fountain for poetic brain
O! My friend all the love for you I retain
Blessed country poet is tied in love chain
In your love O! My friend my head bows
I have feelings............

I have feelings
To you wish to be born and reborn
O! Sindh without you I am lovelorn
Separated from you I am child torn
You my mother to me breeze of morn
Thanks God for my mother Sindh you chose
I have feelings...............

# EXCUSE ME TONIGHT

In Kula lumpur on a busy street
O! Tourist to thee I greet
Tonight I wish to sell myself
For riches and for pelf
Thousands miles away
In a beautiful country far away
To a beautiful mother was born
Unaware of hate, unaware of scorn
For future bright to kula lumpur was drawn
Kula lumpur a city of shine and glamour
Of love, light and sexual demeanor
Here I am a sex worker
Hold my hand come
Mine eyes are fulsome
Supple is body, lithesome
But before you take me to bed
And tear me like husband newlywed
Just for a while listen to me and hear
I am in tears gripped by fear
Before to street I came
My life was not same
I got message my mother died
Before death only to my name she replied
She worried for me and cried
'Daughter' was word before she last sighed
Shattered am I battered am I
On the death of mother tattered am I
"Forget your pain" said my cruel pimp
"Business is business" you shall not wimp

Tonight I am not what I seem
I have, no charm, no lust, no gleam
To you I am not companion right
Please excuse me tonight.

# FEELINGS

I wish to write poetry on a river bank
Alas you are not with me life is blank
River is dried greenery has shrunk
River and me are alone
One without water other by beloved thrown

Stuck in traffic alas I am tired
No imagination, no creativity, lost and fired
Peace and tranquility a dream hay wired
Feeling thoughtless lost and cross fired

In a vision I saw a girl innocent
Looked like little angel her smile sweet
Blushing was she when with me met
Again and again in dreams wish her to greet

You are beautiful and filled with wit
You scorn me and for my love vomit
Your scorn is not for me but for poet
Your hate will not dampen my spirit

At the midnight stars wink at me
Stars! a poetic hindsight blink at me
Stars! like little fairies white prink at me
Milky way full bright for poem thinks at me

I miss my books and my pen
To me hidden truths books explain
Pen writes poems that hook to pain
Books make me free and unchain

Freedom! what a beautiful word you are
A writer's sweet heart, Syed's beloved you are
For the fallen a hope's standard you are
Smile for crestfallen a strong sword you are

Sitting in a garden filled with red roses
Sadness is forbidden gloom deposes
Love feelings widen mirthful smile rises
From within a beautiful vision arises

I am shepherd poverty visible on my face
I sustain severity weep for beloved's disgrace
Come to me O friend, I creep for your solace
Uphill is my pain more and more but not less

Have you ever seen a girl in white dress
A symbol of honour, love, light and grace
I tumble, love feelings unfurl, but find no space
I rumble swept by whirl, wish her to embrace

# SWEET SONGS NEVER DIE

Sweet song of nightingale
You wish to strangle
To you sweet voice is bane
You tuned to flattery plain
But to you let me explain
Even if you are exalted king high
Sweet songs never die

A singer when she sings
Universal bell of freedom rings
To the sleepy her voice stings
Freshness, love, courage song brings
New message of hope song contains
A presage to encourage song retains
Awakened emotions fly high
Sweet songs never die

Last night my house was set ablaze
O! Crazy you laughed for your craze
You thought my all poems are burnt
No more poetry my art is stunt
In the morning I wrote poem new
Poem, drenched in tears looking like dew
Poem, belied your point of view
New poem reflects sobs and sigh
Sweet songs never die

Last night a parrot was killed
With salt his wounds were filled
When he uttered "freedom" it thrilled
He was young, handsome and talented

A popular parrot by all lovingly wanted
From his popularity killer was haunted
Diminished is not the spirit of parrots who fly
Next day flock of parrots were singing battle cry
Sweet songs never die.

# IF DREAMS ARE NOT REALITY

If Dreams are not reality,
But then why they inspire?
With passion they fire?
Dreamers face consequences dire
Dreamers face brute brutality
If dreams are not reality
Then for dreamers why crude cruelty?
If dreams are not reality…………..

If dreams are not reality
If a dreamer says earth is round
And sun is beamer to all stars around
To us, clear secrets of universe astound
Torch bearers, truths universal propound
Sufferings, sufferings, they are burnt to die
Until today human imagination conquers sky
Will, makes way amongst minds dirtiest of dirty
If dreams are not reality……….

If dreams are not reality,
Why my heart yearns for you?
Off and on mind sojourns for you?
At each moment new thought is born for you?
Like a weaver new poem darn for you
Still sapped is not my vitality
If dreams are not reality………..

If dreams are not reality,
I know you will come never
I am not worthy of your favour
Me a goof but not like you clever
You a girl of high society and flavour
Me a son of poor cobbler

But still I believe in merciful pity
If dreams are not reality.............

If dreams are not reality,
Countless years have gone by
Of your hands feel still I feel, why?
Image of thine brings smile thereby
My longing for you a far away cry
 Hope is alive never gone awry
To me your quest is not in futility
If dreams are not reality........

If dreams are not reality,
Why prisoner smiles in torture cell?
Hopeful, even though in hell
Tortured, tormented but down within inner self
Convinced is he of truthfulness of his belief
On bruised lips smile shows virility
If dreams are not reality...........

My friends come let us sing together
For beloved Sindh's bright future
For homeland weave hopes like weaver
Silky, passionate, made of golden fiber
Even if hopes are broken
Our resolve must not be shaken
World renown is our ancient artistry
 If dreams are not reality..........

# WHY ARE YOU NOT COUNTING MY TEARS?

My head is laid under your sword
Killer is waiting for your nod and word
My hands are tied, lips sewed, cries unheard
Silent tears of mine are not seen
My grief is hidden all are down in fear
Why are you not counting my tears?

Amongst crowd silent and hushed
A sound of sob to my ear has rushed
Who is weeping for me when I am crushed?
I feel anguish of some one for my welfare
Is he my son, mother, wife or love of yester years?
Why are you not counting my tears?

Sometimes back in same place I was spectator
To see silted throat of poet who wrote poems spectacular
He a devote to mother tongue refused language of power
In the same night I woke to write first poem for valour
An elegy, a tribute, a salute, in slain poets' honour
Unaware of ugly fate will wait for my writing error
Why are you not counting my tears?

Rest assured no one will speak for us from London
To our ordeal Washington has nothing to be beholden
Continue to steal our land, language, honour and pride
Our wounds will not heal without any mention worldwide
Our fate you will seal, to us your intention is crystal clear
Why are you not counting my tears?

I feel coming days reveal your fate dark to darker
In the killing field I will die on the altar
Seen by wet eyes, pained hearts, emotions welter

Stage is set, energy drained, no one for me to shelter
My hands coughed, my breath huffed, going is a belter
But I know what you don't know about our youngsters
On a poet's death, swords will not be in sheath for fighters
Why are you not counting my tears?

# O! DEATH FOR HOW MANY TIMES YOU WILL KILL ME?

Very much old is story
Of my humiliation and your glory,
I tilled my land and sang songs
Songs of love and hope all along
I was artisan of high calibre
Maker of statue of dancing girl
I was happy in my happy valley
Unaware of the gale pushing me to dark alley
All came to end
I was conquered and enslaved
Crushed, tortured, humiliated
With unending fear you fill me
For how many times O! death you will kill me?

I was captured from Africa like animal
Caged, chained, sold like cattle
My fields taken away
And my women taken to sway
Sufferings, sufferings but no other way
I declared ugly, uncouth, rowdy
By the wielders of gun with uniform tidy
Cut was my tongue
Forbidden either to talk or sing
Not to read words "honour " bring
The day I was caught
Filled with fear pain wrought
Your coming doesn't chill me
For how many times O! death you will kill me?

You killed me in name of religion
For asking questions forbidden
And for the satisfaction of king's passion

With my head minarets have been built
Without any remorse without any guilt
Killers laugh when my throat is slit
I am buried in graves unknown
In whole world under fields still unsown
In the dustbin of history I am thrown
My life, my blood is free for all
For the kings, queens, priests to maul
Is there any to ask why am pushed to wall?
Me a hopeless entity in the world
Desperate to be saved from abuses hurled
Nothing in the world is to thrill me
For how many times O! death you will kill me?

Nowadays I am living in unhappy valley
Where kidnapping is norm killings daily
A hungry witch is unleashed to fill her belly
Witch, thirsty for the blood of handsome young
Young whose dreams and ideals sting
Young bubbling with energy immense
Young grumbling witch's offence
Young for the weak making a defense
In the dead of night comes the witch
Takes away all who dare to ditch
Mothers wail for their sons gone
And sisters beat chest for oppression on
And wives are lost and forlorn
I am poet writing poems against witch hunt
For the weeping mothers and sisters heart burnt
For my poems witch will grill me
For how many times O! death you will kill me?

# LIFE IS A PUZZLE

Sometimes summers' drizzle
Other times frost unbearable
Sometimes smile of child new born
Other times a widows mourn
Sometimes a garden beautiful
Other times a desert rueful
Sometimes a tapestry of Sindhi women
Other times an ugly domain
Sometimes a song of black nightingale
Other times departing lovers wail
Sometimes unbearable journey lengthy
Other times unforgettable moment wealthy
Sometimes hard to live by
Other times a gift lovely hard to deny
With all hustle bustle
Life is a puzzle

O! My friend
Life reveals beauty when holding your hand
And ugliness when before a mean man stand
Your beautiful eyes tell song of classic band
And your hair flowing reveal a rare beauty brand
For every word you utter salute angels wish to send
But strange is life flow
Sometimes fast sometimes slow
Life burdensome I lose your beauty's glow
Lonely nights, me, tears and wet pillow
Song of eyes lost in travelling water shallow
All is not well but muddle
Life is a puzzle

O! My friend
Life is tearful when a mother cries for dying baby
A baby who died in the hands of doctors careless shabby
A baby victim of hungry politicians pitiless greedy
Life horrible when a girl killed in name of honour
Terrible when a father drowns his beautiful daughter
My country men living in poverty, killing like monster
Downtrodden's cry neither moving earth nor sky
Drunkard rulers corrupt, to my men honourable life deny
But all of sudden a daffodil grows
A young man for suffering people to gallows goes
Crushed are awakened and trust they repose
In the tears hope comes for the morose
Dying hero's smile is a riddle
Life is a puzzle.

# O! MY LORD

Listen to me O! my Master
You were master of my father and his fore fathers
For unknown generations you were our godfather
Before we ate, your name recited by our mother
Your word law for us O! mighty ruler
We stood, we sat down when received your order
Our tongues impure if not sang in your honour
But tonight O! my mighty listen to son of a cobbler
I have to tell you a very strange tale
I have seen blood on your trail I have seen a nasty rebel
A pauper, a tall, lanky, frail
He speaks against you O! my feeder
He asks questions "Why people wail"
Tortured, pushed to hell
O! My king his questions if allowed
Will empower still mellowed
Kingdom will come down
People will kick your crown

O! My lord, mighty, powerful
To ask question was not allowable
A lesson you taught us valuable
To question you, a feat intolerable
Your fear has been broken
Today a rebel has risen
Old order he has shaken
Care for your rule not taken
People he tries to enlighten
New thought to your subjects given
O! My lord a trend has set in
Even my mind has waken

I have begun to feel and smile
Unworthy thoughts of a virile
Sometimes feeling cruelty of your style
Other time making you a hostile
O! lord stop new thought
Otherwise down you will be brought

My lord why your face is stiffening?
Why my lord, I feel you weakening?
Have you seen your reckoning?
Do you see your end beckoning?
If true and yes
Be brave say with grace
You ruled only to debase
You were a ruler filled with mess
A tyrant nothing to harness
On earth a shame and disgrace
Before your crown crumbles down
I want to tell you a secret hitherto unknown
The rebel who will bring you down
Is son of mine O! Lord tumbling down
I feel happy or shall be shaky?
A father of rebel or subject of king freaky?
I don't know why?
My heart is thumping with joy
On the fall of king, I don't want to cry.

# TO YOU WHAT ELSE SHALL I CALL?

Sindh O! my lovely mother land
Love of pious rishis of Rigved
For thousands years towering you stand
You our holy mother we children grand
To me eternal love my childlike enthrall
To you what else shall I call ?

Dokri town of love and liberty
Of Brave youngsters multi variety
To us you a gift of divinity
You mother to civilization of creativity
In the whole world my love above all
To you what else shall I call?

O! Rome European city of light
Lush green, luminous, shining, bright
You a witness of ancient humans' might
Glorious you are hub of free thought
To poets, painters, thinkers protective wall
To you what else shall I call?

O! my wise graceful mother
In honour of your painful labour
Apposite words fail to write or utter
You an epitome of grace and honour
On my heart your name wish to scrawl
To you what else shall I call?

O! my wife lovely graceful
To me you are the most beautiful
Girl dashing, superb, skilful
Without you my life zero nil
You my strength if I fall
To you what else shall I call?

TO YOU WHAT ELSE SHALL I CALL?

Makka my friend where are you?
I have roses and rose petals for you
O lovely girl for your talent I adore you
Thou are poetic inspiration I swore you
You a girl of wonder I recall
To you what else shall I call?

My country men bare footed
For rulers an entity to be looted
Rise O! Sons of soils be counted
For those who stood and resisted
History has place tallest of tall
To you what else shall I call?

# LIFE STILL I AM LOVER OF THINE

With all your crudity
Torture torments and absurdity
Wisdom vanishing with reigning stupidity
Poor's life darkening in burgeoning poverty
With all your, nudity, vulgarity and tricks dirty
But every breath within me creates tempest
Emotions, within me commotion, I feel warmest
Spirit high,dirty feelings deny, I feel embrace sweetest
To me you are like bride wed newly
Confused, charming, faltering, but fair and lovely
O! Life you are a master artful not a concubine
O! Life still I am lover of thine

If I am spurned for my love so what
If You are mourned for somersault
If I am under your memories' assault
Yet I am hopeful in all times
In union, in separation, about beautiful dimes
To me hopelessness is great crime of all crimes
My poems are for lovers brave
Shun grief, tears never save
Hope is my unfaltering lifeline
O! Life still I am lover of thine

Still sun rises from east
Moonlight begets thoughts sweet
Blooming of flowers, a message to interpret
Long hair of a damsel for a poet cause to celebrate
On the first cry of child new born

Forgotten is pain by mother worn
In cradle smiling baby playful
Hopes waddle, a new message for hopeful

In sweltering heat, I feel covered under sunshine
O! Life still I am lover of thine

Outside the door still I wait
You will meet we will celebrate
Years have passed prolonged is wait
Door will open my hope not to abate
Your long hair golden coloured
Molten was my heart on hair unfurled
Rose coloured face of thine
Once in life, grace to see, I pine
My lips still feel the taste of kiss
Wisps of thine still I miss
Even if stars loose shine
O! sweet heart I will wait for thine
O! Life still I am lover of thine

I remember parting painful
A cloudy cool day gainful
You were leaving I was strain full
Your hug warm made me joyful
But now longing is unbearable
I miss you O! My friend fashionable
Lovely, gracious, beauty unbelievable
On the break of every dawn
Stark realities to me spawn
In the hands of fate dark, me a pawn
Will we meet? seems never
But hope beams to me for far ever
If reality is bleak, dreams are clear
Every night in dress bright you appear
With my dreams I am fine
O! Life still I am lover of thine.

# WHAT IS DIFFERENCE
# BETWEEN YOU AND US?

You a rising star we twilight
Ours life fading, yours lovely bright
Is there a difference, huge between us?
Of what? race, religion, colour or status?

Is colour of your blood different than mine?
Is your smile different and tears with unique sign?
Do you laugh in grief and in fit of happiness weep?
For you darkness is brief for us long and deep?

On death you will turn into flower petals?
We into dust dirty which never settles?
We humans mindless you clever beetle?
Reckless are we and you with flair of battles?

For our forefathers earning livelihood a battle hard
For your forefathers living prince hood, title lord
Ours death is lampooned, on your death sing bards
Death is death but for us curse and for you a reward

If I am poet, is writing poems fault of mine?
Aren't the roles for all humans defined by divine
Creators life is in damns, for other all riches shine
For one, life a hymn, for us no pleasure to combine

If you are beautiful, we ugly, whose fault is this?
Do you know drops of dew plant everywhere kiss
To all moonlight enchants, ensures none to miss
And smell of flowers goes, for all not to amiss

Will you do us a favour? learned man clever
Stop thinking of being saviour, you an aggressor
Happiness of ours you devour, O! transgressor
Since centuries for life better we yearn and clamour.

# FLAG

Battle was fierce
Between invaders and landowners
Moans, groans, slogans of soldiers
Dead bodies filled the battlefield
Every side trying to show power they wield
All of sudden battle begun to take a turn
Land owners weaken, falling one by one
Before sun set out,
land owners faced rout
Landowners leader torn and worn
Body bruised but spirit unworn
In one hand held sword in other flag
Until flag was upheld hope was not to sag
Time was short task was high
How to ensure? flag continued to fly
Worn leader looked up in the sky
Tears rolled down he began to cry
O! God I am not afraid to die
But if our flag lowers down
My people will falter down
On the ground before I fall
Onslaught of invaders stall
Before you take my soul away
Ours flag shall not fall in anyway

Before leader crumbled down
With arrows his body strewn
Falling down was he slowly slowly
Holding tightly, flag not to go lowly lowly
For a miracle to happen all of sudden
His prayers answered by power hidden
From a corner of battlefield, a boy came
Tall, thin, weak without any strong frame

From the hands of falling leader
Flag he took away and became carrier
Right in the centre of chest
In the midst of heart, flag he vests
Fastly high cliff he climbed
Falling leader looked up and smiled
To fly high, by boy, flag was primed
So sudden was all action
Invaders shocked and felt browbeaten
They knew if flag was not to remove
Fruitless all efforts for victory will prove
Angry were they battle had slipped away
Quickly they surrounded hill
To bring down flag, proved task uphill

Legend says flag still high stands
Onslaught of invaders, still withstands
For centuries war is going on
Brutality of invaders growing on
But landowners are not tumbling down
On chest landowners' youngsters flag paste
Attempt of invaders falters and goes waste
Flag is symbol of hope
Hope invaders can't dope
Hope invaders can't rope
Hope invaders can't cope
For landowners hope can't elope.

# MISSING PERSON

Up in sky or below under earth
Broken body, breath loose worth
Motionless as if baby in still birth
Is he dead or alive? is unknown truth
He is hated seen with aversion
Probably he is a missing person

In a smelly, dirty, dingy cell
For last four years he is in hell
His mind is numbed thoughts stale
He neither smiles nor tries to wail
Neither he cries nor averse to aspersion
Probably he is a missing person

Four years ago, he was twenty years old
Young strong aplenty with stares unsold
A village girl of shanty, adored his mould
A damsel of twenty, stored hope for his fold
Memory is lost today unaware of life stern
Probably he is a missing person

Four years ago, one day, he on his way
Was taken in vehicle grey, so people say
Rumours say he went stray, found a ray
A ray of hope disliked by men in uniform grey
Punished was he for daring diversion
Probably he is a missing person

Four years ago, when he was picked
Broken were ribs when with boots kicked
Taken was tongue by the tall man wicked
Teeth ripped, body burnt, cigarettes stubbed
Nothing is left of him but man's version
Probably he is a missing person.

# HYPOCRISY

My father slept with a woman cleaner
And my mom seduced a boy driver
And my sister had an extra marital affair
But when I have fallen in love with a son of driver
My decision to marry has shaken my mother
Sadness my father is unable to bear
In posh bungalow in defense we live
High priority to high status we give
Rubbish for high society is all
If on their standard doesn't fall
And what are the standards?
Truth, honesty, are sub-standards
Simplicity not to be tendered
Big cars and dresses branded
For daughters grooms rich demanded
Groom rich, even if bastard, not minded
In the society hypocrite
Filled with hoary lies white
To make my parents happy
I to leave my love and live unhappy
Love of son of driver
My craze my mentor
Will I be able to forget him?
And curse myself for all life to come?

# O! GOD WHAT HEART YOU GAVE ME?

O! God what heart you gave me?
Beauties kill and rave me
I feel lost, I feel drowned, save me
You are Lord, but your people misbehave me
Me a bard, love and yearnings enslave me

Other day I was in corridor of power
Everyone hassling for flattery of leader
Agenda for poor was seen nowhere
They laughed, talked but not about future
Feelings sad from within crave me
O! God what heart you gave me?

All the day long I dabble in files
Files, filled with tears, miseries, cries
To Sindh happiness ruler denies
Agony of mine in the day touches skies
Painful is night, pains, they have me
O! God what heart you gave me?

How shall I describe pain of mothers?
Ailing husband's, children in tatters
Agony, each passing day furthers
Looming vultures for grown up daughters
Mountains of sadness brave me
O! God what heart you gave me?

For all day long thoughts throng
From where am I, to where belong?
Somewhere something is wrong
My land, my people crushed by strong
Miseries wildly wave at me
O! God what heart you gave me?

Life is to pass with all zigzags in anyway
With tags of good way, bad way, either way
But alas my homeland is sad being taken away
My mother tongue is hamstrung and torn away
How shall I live? A new way pave me
O! God what heart you gave me?

O! My beloved where have you gone?
Candle in my hand search for you on
If you meet me again, I will be reborn
Beautiful flower love is, not a thorn
From ordeal, come and save me
O! God what heart you gave me?

# EVERY TIME I FALL IN LOVE NEW

Every time I fall in love new
Dressing changes, hair take style new
Eyes speak and lips take turn new
Universe sings a song absolutely new
For lover changes whole world view
Every time I fall in love new

Every moment poetry befriends me
A beautiful girl, God sends me
A new poem whirls and bends to me
A poetic gem, a vision new stands me
Whims of mine find a mission new
Every time I fall in love new

Sometimes I am shunned by you
Other times I am burned by you
O! youth prime I am spurned by you
O! Girl sublime I am returned by you
For lovers this view is not new
Every time I fall in love new

Years ago, when you came to me
Tearful were you, plight same to me
Careful were you, height of acclaim to me
Unforgettable were you, all life that came to me
Blessed was I with beautiful view
Every time I fall in love new

When I say 'I love you'
You say 'I respect your point of view'
Between these we say words a few
Storms we suppress that within us brew
Who else about our hearts knew?
Every time I fall in love new

Behind every smile I have mountains of pain
Torture, torments, stains I have to sustain
Yet from heart in strains flows love fountain
Your name is written on my soul on brain
For your lost love, my life is under review
Every time I fall in love new

Every morning in the summers hot
My heart bleeds and is grief wrought
In the nights hot sleep gone in thoughts
Unbearable and hotter is memory's onslaught
I am a soul never off your purview
Every time I fall in love new

In nights wintry long and cold
Universe in slumber, my wounds unfold
Thought's blabber, at pains' threshold
Me a jilted lover barely breath hold
For every night my wounds renew
Every time I fall in love new

Years ago, suddenly a girl came my way
Speechless was she unable to anything say
Pain is my name haltingly she could say
For her end was horribly gone stray
What a pity for love like dew
Every time I fall in love new.

# MONSTERS

I tell her a lie
I love you when I say with sigh
Good actor I am
Easy for me to bring girl into love frame
I have no remorse no shame
For every month three
I wish to get rid and be free
From the girl who came to me
It is symbol of my manhood
To rob chastity like Robin Hood
To fleece women's woman hood
Who can dare to challenge me?
Is anyone ready to face revenge of me?
I am mighty powerful
With prowess wonderful
If someone calls me monster
Rude image of mine it bolsters,
I damn care for people's voices
Loathsome, ugly, dirty novices
I loath who don't follow me
With praise and power wallow me
Still humanity in east is far away
From the truth of glorious day
People have courage to say
Monsters are monsters, people shall say
Monsters are monsters, people shall say.

# STRANGE INCIDENT.

Last night to me strange incident happened
My twenty years old radiant glasses misshapened
Gone was old vision brilliant a new world envisioned
I saw timid as a valiant and valiant's face blackened
Buoyant was gradient, brave was threatened
Light turned black, radiant turned into irradiant
Last night to me strange incident happened

A strange world unfolded and seemed to me
Viciousness, cruelty, scolded and beamed to me
A girl in the hands of father for help screamed to me
She was taken to brothel thought streamed to me
Was it poverty, quest for status or self respect lessened?
Last night to me strange incident happened

For a girl years ago in the nights I wept
Eyes wet with tears strife within I felt
A dream in tatters, pain rife, her picture I kept
Life like misers, strain around me wrapt
Tonight all seemed feelings of a man harkened
Last night to me strange incident happened

Strange is world, writers bow before power
For cursed, poems are written praise they shower
Sage and saintly is called a bloody corrupt ruler
Untrue is adage 'from sword pen is mightier'
But tonight, I see power is shaken and weakened
Last night to me strange incident happened

Years ago me a son of cobbler was alone
Harsh was life no pity, no mercy was shown
Borrowed books my friends, rags were worn
Insults were hurled, my respect was thrown
But now by calls of beauties I am awakened
Last night to me strange incident happened

For years a feudal lord raped girls of peasants
He thought himself a powerful god omnipresent
To him all the girls of subjects were godly present
He used, he abused, he giggled, cruelty incessant
To night he pimped his daughter to save his future darkened
Last night to me strange incident happened

I doubt my poems are any clarion call
Will they make any dent in power's hall?
Will they raise for crushed any protective wall?
Onslaught of oppressors, will they stall?
Yet to me poetry makes my resolve hardened
Last night to me strange incident happened.

# AT TWENTY-FIVE AGE.

At twenty-five age
Within me love dreams rage
Broken is cage, emotions rage
Crossed are all Shakespearean stages
I think, world at brink, me only sage
At twenty five age

To me everything is a joke
Anything I can make and revoke
Amongst dead life I can evoke
Fire in hearts I can stoke
Strange powers within me rage
At twenty five age

To me every girl is butterfly
Sigh of lover is moon in sky
My love is power none deny
For my love sky isn't limit to fly
For me life thy name is courage
At twenty five age

Each and every passing day
To my ideals homage I pay
Amongst odds I find new way
For me, exists no area grey
Immense courage to fight savage
At twenty five age

Fatigue is unknown to me
Always new ways are shown to me
Word 'no' is not known to me
Greatness within is sown to me
I am young man on world stage
At twenty five age

To me ocean is small stream
High Mountain a bubble of steam
Under heat I feel shadow of neem
Sweeter is the taste of world, ice cream
I stand against all wild rampage
At twenty five age

To me every poem is for my beloved
lines of prose for my beloved are chilled
Twinkling of stars for my beloved are willed
By name of my beloved moonlight is thrilled
Gust of wind for my beloved a presage
At twenty-five age

To me wintry nights are short
And long days of June just start
My dreams my visions are smart
My hopes no one can distort
I am bubbling at point vintage
At twenty five age.

# REBELLION

You question my integrity
My qualification my honesty
To you I am a non entity
Created to play to your tunes
Say words who you to attune
From all faults you are immune
And I am sinner since time unknown
But remember I am also a human
With blood, bones, feelings, emotions
Your words hurt me
Your arrogance insults me
My silence is not acceptance
Your piercing words put me at askance

You are proud of English excellent
And jeer at my rustic accent
Remember I am son of soil
I get meal if I struggle and toil
You suck blood of ours
Beginning with our ancestors
But time is changing fast
Narrowing is world vast
Pall of doom on your fate is cast
Slaves have woken up
Dream of freedom taken up
Standing before you with lowered eyes
And tied hands on chest and hushed sighs
Is not reflection of our subjugation
But burning heart with raging emotions

Mentally free are we
No more beholden to thee
Dawn from us is a niche away
Chains we will throw away
Hope you can't snatch away
Crown of your's we will take away.

# I CAN'T SAY HAPPY NEW YEAR

At midnight twelve, clock will click
Hearts throb, lovers, glasses will pick
Drum beats, firing and jolly voices thick
Vows will grow and promises to stick
But here in my homeland valley unhappy
Polluted by rulers filthy and shabby
New dawn will not harbinger a new hope
In darkness we will continue to grope
My eyes will be filled with fear
How can I say happy new year?

In my homeland darkness will deepen
Hope for bright new dawn will lessen
Punishment harsh for us will be chosen
Poverty, hunger, injustice will threaten
My homeland will be drenched in blood
O! My friends living around the world
On the advent of new year, you are thrilled
Accept greetings from your friend poet hack
for the pain of homeland, he weeps without break
My eyes are filled with sadness and tears
How can I say happy new year?

For us every year gory stories are same,
Fraud is everywhere democracy a sham
Our aspirations everyday burnt, put aflame
Our fate miserable, rulers show no remorse, no shame
We the subjects just be played like cards' game
To raise head a crime and question, wrath to inflame
Fine brains sublime killed on flimsy blame
Suffocation, tension, worries name of life became
Corruption, assassinations is the name of game

For such a life miserable without hope without thrill
Life is unbearable, to write a poem of happiness, unthinkable
Agony of my homeland who else will bear?
How can I say happy new year?

At the eve of new year, I wish to a girl send flower
Grow roses with fragrance before they deflower
Write poems with thoughts new whistle blower
About love, life, dance, wine and cheerful lovers
for a poet hack for hope to continue to flicker
Some light must come to my heart as shower
But lamentations of my land to me unbearable
Dashed are hopes when I see a weeping mother
And for the missing brother a crying sister
And a girl killed in the name of family honour
And my land taken by a cruel usurper
At all times anguish to me continuously whisper
In the sleepless nights and restless days
A poet from the East to all friends says
Cross of pain of my homeland is on my shoulder
Your happiness on new year I will not be able to share
How can I say happy new year?

# HEADACHE I HAVE TONIGHT

Headache I have tonight
To stop tears with emotions I fight
I feel I am walking on rope tight
Will I be able to my fight rewrite?
Turning my bleak present into future bright?
Headache I have tonight.

Long time ago a soothsayer told me
Strange world will unfold to me
Idea of greatness he sold to me
But now strange notions hold me
As if blood has turned from red to white
Headache I have tonight.

Something is terribly wrong here
Non-entities are invariably strong here
Hoarse voices unbearably sing song here
To teaching profession illiterates belong here
What poem shall I write?
Headache I have tonight.

A doctor sells medicine for fortune good
Prescription is expensive, cheap he could
Offered is he trip by Pharma, to Europe he would
Least is care for patients, otherwise proper he should
Stories of corruption I need to write and rewrite
Headache I have tonight.

End is near in the twilight of life
Inner self is filled with restlessness and strife
To be in love new with passion in age ripe
Hard is it, old tension free role to swipe
To discard emotions new for how much time will fight?
Headache I have tonight.

Money, money, money endless is quest
But who will stop race at my behest?
Piety is found cloaked in shameless heist
Power is slave to brazen less dishonest
Cries of dying are way-less to the height
Headache I have tonight.

For all my poems filled with tearful sorrow
From where shall cheerfulness I borrow?
My self-pity, heart empty, fearful to bury in burrow
Let me become a poet artful to hide pain thorough
Till tonight painful is noose of slavery tight
Headache I have tonight.

I can't live fully life of my own
From childhood up to mature man grown
Enveloped in worries gauntlets at me thrown
For every fleeting second, by life no mercy shown
For my siblings I am worried for their poor plight
Headache I have tonight.

For all the day I wait to hear something soothing
A smile of beauty, a sonorous voice heart moving
Tensionless life, colourful rainbow up showing
A natural blade that sorrows, worries, mowing
Endless is quest for life forthright
Headache I have tonight.

# LOVE AT SEA-VIEW

Long silky hair below shoulders
Passers by fall in love then and there
Crimson is face, wind plays with her
Waves are coming to behold her
For the happenings around she is unaware

A poet of romance and hope stands nearby
In trance, unaware girl ropes him thereby
Stance of girl lovely makes him sad and cry
For the memory of beloved of days gone by
A gift of poem shakes him not to stand by

Ocean is silent and sun is slowly slowly falling
A jilted lover on the sand name of beloved scrawling
From the minaret of mosque a muezzin is calling
A child is running to mother with joy gamboling
A girl beauty stunning is pleasing like snowballing
Poets' heart is running crossing all fences and walling

If cloud covers sun, is earth happy or sad?
On touch tender, why beautiful face is red?
Of a piety pretender, why his heart is crude?
Love is not for bystander, a poet has said
Ocean of fire is love, only brave can wade
O girl beautiful to you salutations I send

Holding hands two lovers stroll on beach
Love love love from every corner is screech
Live in the moment inner voice is within reach
Immersed is universe for love songs to preach
Damn to moral code, for love, let us breach
We the lovers a new song to world will teach

A saint is sitting on the walls of beach view
before him stands a poet who has fallen in love new
He has son, beautiful wife life free from tensions too
Off guard was he, when new love feelings grew
Every moment love for wife and son for him renew
Fatal is attraction, how will he sustain injury new?

Is hope a boon or bane, if a heart filled with strain?
What is difference between sane and an inane?
One is torn by wisdom, other locked by a folly chain?
Unploughed land is also land but ploughed filled with grain?
Coloured cloth hides blot but white shows visible stain
Standing on a beach, in emotional stretch feel in new terrain.

# WILL YOU BELIEVE?

Will you believe?
In a country of pious
Duplicity is obvious
Honesty on the run
All is for wielder of gun
Fire, ointment for burn
People are like turtle
Hidden heads of mortal
New ideas crushed to unfurl
For them who will grieve?
Will you believe?

A parrot is called crow
And donkey a cow
Books are called mess
Ignorance a form of grace
Reading a source of stress
Locked are minds at birth
And lies are sold as truth
Holy cows are all powerful
Above law, to none answerable
No pill for pain to relieve
Will you believe?

Whole generation of a nation
Have adopted to a fashion
Improve life standard by corruption
Money earned by illegal means
Used to fulfil all the ignoble dreams

Dreams, where beautiful girls are chased
Dreams, where luxury cars are purchased
Dreams, where wine has supremacy
Dreams, where going to west is fantasy
For poor no hope no reprieve
Will you believe?

# I HAVE LOST KEYS

I have lost keys; my memories are inside
Memories of what? Of my life's darker side?
For forty-eight years long
Of my rooms everything belonged
I wept when I was wronged
And felt amazed a man strong
On smile of her, who for me was never
Illusions made me happy
Delusions illustrated my fake identity
For many I was man noble
A writer with outlook global
But to her a man meaningless
My words to her shameless
Me a man grace less
I knock at memory-door
Try to recall what is indoor?
Dementia, I feel washed is memory floor
I go to a man wise
To seek his advice
Why is tricky memory lane?
Sometimes filled, sometimes plain?
I wish to walk along old alley
Probably of my last birth's valley
But I am lost
To do something, but what?
I have lost my keys; my memories are inside
Keys? I think I never had
Keys? I think were my illusion bad
Keys? Never existed, I am afraid
For now I am lost I am sad.

# O! MY BELOVED

In far off mountains Sun dips low
Hurrying to kiss beloved waiting below
Trying to honour loyalty vow
Me too come from far off land
Made of mountains, river, ocean,sand
Kiss your hair, dimples and feet
My action till resurrection I will repeat

In a sweltering sunny noon
Standing on a burning dune
As the grains of sand shine
I feel you singing under tree of wine
Now desert turning into heaven
O! My beloved you are chosen by divine
You are my nectar is proven

O! My beloved me from a land
Greetings through moon we send
In the night in dazzling light
Walking in street moonlit bright
If you feel tender touch on cheek
On your lips trickles smile meek
Moonlight is kissing you for lover freak.

# O! MY SUN!

O my Sun!
To you I am sunflower
To bow to you I turn everywhere
Since time unknown
I wait for your mercy to be shown
But wait is unbearably long
To thee I belong
I decay, I dwindle, I burn O my Sun!

O my Sun!
Your love-thoughts puzzle me
Your separation sizzles me
With your light, come, dazzle me
With your wit, come, drizzle me
My emotions for you are as a whole
To see you, mine last wish last goal
Destiny, for me you have fixed what a role!
Wait wait wait wait until goes away my soul
O! dazzling light eternal, come, not to spurn
O! My Sun

O my Sun!
Burn me to ashes
Like falling star crashes
But bestow me power of Phoenix
Who raises from his own ashes
From the ashes when I raise
My all poetry shall be in your praise
To thee I belong, tag to me stays
People may say it a poetic hyperbole
But to me it is gist of my soul
Come, come, come time will turn
O! My Sun

O my Sun!
If a garden is filled with flowers
But a bee over a certain flower hovers
Attention is drawn by only honey-power
To me your glimpse of beauty beam
Has bestowed me with high esteem
I am drawn to your beautiful gleam
To your smile a cascading flow
And your laughter heartening glow
To you I owe all poetic glory
In your love if I die, I will not be sorry
To me you are nectar for heart sunken
O! My Sun.

# WHY I DANCE?

On the eighteenth birthday of mine
I am dancing before you O! sons of swine
You are jeering at me and splashing wine
Ah! Your cry for my clothes to say goodbye
I a paid dancer, how your wish can deny?
You wish, before you, I undress
To your eyes my body shall bless
To you, your power and money
Make you lusty and hungry
O! Ye so called elite of country
A country bastion of hypocrisy
Corrupt, dishonest with mind dirty
To us your power and money
Is, neither sweet nor honey
I dance to earn my livelihood
Broken, at sale of my youth hood
You yearn to eat my flesh
Every part of my body you clash
My smile to you
Willingness of mine, you construe
Behind my smile is hidden pain
Of a daughter under strain
Of a sister, of whose body
Is sold to fight hunger bloody
Before you I smile and dance
You think I am happy and in trance
From the deepest core of heart, I loathe
Your lust, your sex-thirst, your jeer, your cheer
As my loathe grows stronger
My feet become warmer
To hide my anger
I dance, I dance, I dance
To avoid your dirty glance
Dance for avoiding pain is my only chance.

# CYCLE OF LIFE

I eat
I sleep
I talk
I work
And one day I will die
Is it cycle of life?

But before I die
To write a poem, I wish
Meaningful, deep, stylish
After my death readers cherish
To me immortality it bestows
All creative power of mine it shows

But before I die
To the girl, once I wish to meet
Who was lovey beautiful and sweet
She loved me, she claimed
One day she left, I felt ashamed
For three long years I wept for her
Still deep hurt I have of her rude behaviour
One question I just want to ask
For three years, I struggled for pain to mask
Wisest of wise say
Remembrance is traffic two way
For all the years long
At any moment, did my memory to you throng?
If no, then I shall say wisest of wise are wrong

But before I die
I wish to meet all the women I admire
Beautiful, talented, my poetry they inspire
Before death takes me to unbreakable slumber
To the beauties I wish to tell

'Gems are you', I wish to say in nutshell
Some of yours flowing hair
And some others skilful flair
And some of others bodily flare
All were my poetic inspiration
Source of my creative transformation

But before I die
I wish the dream of my father to fulfil
To send me to best university was his will
To fulfil his dream, is my dream still
To reach at Oxford, still I till
My father a poor man
A poet, a scholar of high domain
He taught me, poverty teaches forbearance
He taught me to keep hopes high and aloft
If you are alone, if you are poor so what?
All success of mine to him I owe
Dearth of words, for him respect to show
I wish to honour his memory
By breaking shackles of slavery

But before I die
I wish to see Sindh my chained home land
A country free, respected amongst nations stands
I wish to see respect for all religions is shown
Bigotry, hatred be words for coming generations unknown
My country Sindh is a model state
Where each and every one is respected and great
Ignorance is wiped out of slate
To write English biography
Of Saen, without hagiography
A scholar, a Sindh's saviour
To show my love for the great leader

# O MY FRIEND!

O my friend!
Do you remember the night cold?
We like birds free, in flying mood
Tick tick of time we ignored
Each other's arms we adored
With our steps earth jerked
In each other we merged

O my friend!
First night, to each other, we strangers
But in the first glance, we felt trance
Our eyes met, attraction hidden we felt
All of sudden, a long journey is done
We take to Floor, voices say en core en core
In the middle of night, we are lovers bright

O my friend!
Let us plant roses together
Black, white, red of all colours
Let us drink from cup of eternity
Of love, togetherness and serenity
Let us earn and celebrate our immortality
With our love great and unsnapped vitality

O my friend!
In a full moon night standing alone
Moon in full glory, all stars outshone
Star one Only, is against moon-glory
Star is drowned in its own beauty-story
It all reminds of your beauty impeccable
Soothing, glorified, continuity unchangeable

O my friend!
Today I saw picture of thine
Where are you? For you I pine?
Come to me I will take you under tree of wine
You a flower me a honey- bee
O! life allow me once to see
In embrace of my friend and be happy

O my friend!
Tonight in mid dream I woke up
In an strange stream I broke up
To an unknown land I was flying
Overtaken by yearning I was dying
Far beloved far away I was crying
Grief of mine angels were enjoying

O my friend!
Glory will be thine if I die
I will live in heart of thy
For you l leave a book of verses
Do you believe? Each poem to you refers
Tears will wet your beautiful eyes
Existence of mine to you poem reminds.

# ACKNOWLEDGEMENTS

My sincere thanks to my wife Arifa who was instrumental to help me in writing this book. I am highly indebted to love and encouragement of fellow students at University of Rome Tor, Vergata, especially my sisters Rim and Sania, my brother Sharif and my loving friend Makka. To my beautiful beloved friend Aina, who is an immense source of creative inspiration. Last but not least team of Author house and my dear friend Aziz Mangi, without whose efforts publication of this book would not have been possible.

# ABOUT THE AUTHOR

Dadlo Zuhrani was born on 27th May 1971 in a small village "Dino Wahan" near Dokri Town, District Larkana, Sindh, Pakistan, situated on the bank of Dadu Canal, surrounded by beautiful natural scenes, green fields, orchards and sweet songs of birds. In spite of the natural beauty and lovely environment, the poet also went through curse of poverty, backwardness, helplessness, oppression, tyranny, exploitation and torment of life. Combo of beauty and poverty equally inspired Dadlo for writing short stories and novels in his mother tongue Sindhi and poetry in English. His writings reflect beauty, Struggle and bitter social realities.

In 2016, his Novel in Sindhi language "Dunya Dam Darya" was published and declared best novel of the year by Sindhi Language Authority, and Literary Association of Progressive Writers.

Being a poet of romance and harsh social realities, Dadlo Zuhrani writes whatever he personally sustains or observes. His poetry truly reflects the woes and pains of downtrodden and oppressed peoples. His poetry is full of deep thoughts, poetic sensitivity and beauty.

Dadlo Zuhrani is Civil Servant by profession and he has done his International Master in Public Procurement Management (IMPPM) from University of Rome, Tor, Vergata.

Printed in the United States
by Baker & Taylor Publisher Services